FIELD HOCKEY

PHYSICAL EDUCATION ACTIVITIES SERIES

Consulting Editor:
AILEENE LOCKHART
University of Southern California
Los Angeles, California

Evaluation Materials Editor:
JANE A. MOTT
Smith College
Northampton, Massachusetts

PHYSICAL EDUCATION

ACTIVITIES SERIES

FIELD HOCKEY

ANNE LEE DELANO

Smith College
Northampton, Massachusetts

Illustrated by **JEAN PUTNAM**

WM. C. BROWN COMPANY PUBLISHERS
DUBUQUE, IOWA

Printed in U. S. A.

Preface

This book was written for the student with little or no field hockey experience. Its purpose is to present as many of the facets of the game as possible within the space allotted. As the various techniques are described the rules are interspersed because the two are so intertwined. Generalities for both attack and defense play, practice suggestions, and specific information for forwards, halfbacks, fullbacks and the goalkeeper are included in order to answer at least some of the questions of the reader, and to increase the understanding of both the participant and the observer.

Self-evaluation questions are included throughout the text so that the student can test herself in typical kinds of understanding and levels of skill that she should be acquiring. The reader should not only answer the printed questions but should invent additional ones as a self-check on progress.

The control, discipline, alertness and reaction time, and basic principles of movement demanded by this game are required in many activities and thus cannot help having carry-over values, regardless of the specific sports in which one may engage in the future. It is impossible to put into words the openness and speed of field hockey, but these should become more evident as techniques and positional play are mastered.

Contents

Introduction to Field Hockey

THE GAME

Field hockey is played in many countries by both men and women. No book can fully describe its excitement which extends from the moment you have first learned to receive and control the ball to the privilege of representing your country here and abroad. It is an exhilarating game which fulfills the love of being out of doors, sometimes regardless of the weather, and the enjoyment of running, though how much depends upon the position you choose to play.

Each team consists of eleven players: five forwards, three halfbacks, two fullbacks and a goalkeeper. Each defense player has an immediate opponent whom she is determined will not score a goal. The side halfbacks are responsible for the wings, the fullbacks for the inners, and the center halfback for the center forward. At the beginning of the game, after each goal is scored and at the beginning of the second half, the players line up on either side of the center line on a field that is 90 to 100 yards long and 50 to 60 yards wide. The game is started by a bully between the two opposing center forwards, and on its completion the forwards may and should cross the line prepared to receive a pass and to open up the space between attack and defense. In order to score a goal (one point), the ball must be hit or at least touched by the stick of an attack player within the striking circle.

The challenge of the game and its techniques are based on the simple fact that only the flat side of the stick may be used. A player must become flexible, particularly through the shoulders, and agile, able to move in

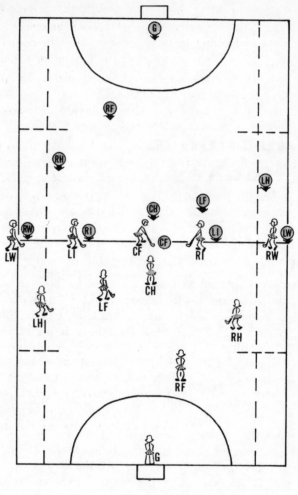

Figure 1

any direction at varying speeds; quick off the mark yet with the control and balance necessary to stop and turn at will. In the execution of all techniques there are three restrictions. No part of the stick may come above shoulder level ("sticks"). Second, no part of one's body may come between one's opponent and the ball if the opponent is within reach of the ball ("obstruction"). Last, one may not advance or move the ball in any direction with any part of the body, the one exception being the goalkeeper who uses her feet more than her stick.

For any infringement of these rules outside the striking circles, a free hit is awarded to the opposing team. If the infringement occurs within the circle by the defending team, a short or penalty corner is awarded; if by the attack, a free hit is awarded to the defending team.

The offside rule limits set patterns and plays. No player in her attacking half of the field may be *ahead* of the ball when it is hit by one of her own team unless there are three defenders between her and the goal. The goalkeeper is included in this count of three.

Hockey is a game of masterful skill and deception, anticipation and concentration, a game where five forwards are determined to score, backed up by three halfbacks who can and should shoot for goals. Learning to outwit an opponent, to capitalize on an opponent's mistake, to recover quickly when your team is on the defense are characteristics which make the game exciting. When you are the player farthest from the ball on a field which is 100 yards long and can still be in the game mentally as well as physically, preparing for the move which is about to happen, then you will have attained that quality which will make hockey the sport which can offer so much to your pleasure. As in any game, no situation will ever be completely duplicated and no one can tell you what to do in every situation.

Together with the skill of handling yourself, your stick and the ball, there are the intangibles for which you are aiming: alertness, cooperation, the ability to think and act quickly and decisively, to adjust to a situation calmly with control, and to develop a sympathy and an empathy with each member of your team as each tries to perform her task. These are the satisfactions which will make you look forward to playing hockey for many years to come.

2

Basic Techniques

Although you probably will have played hockey many times before you have mastered or even used all of the skills described in this chapter, the situations you will have faced may be at least partially solved as you read, practice and understand these basic techniques. How to hold your stick, to dribble, to drive, how to dodge an opponent and to retrieve a ball from her are all explained.

Practicing in slow motion is of little value. Always *work for maximum speed with control*. By so doing you will increase your endurance and also begin to match the tempo of a game.

What you wear should be graceful in appearance and allow freedom of movement. Rubber cleated shoes are desirable for quick starts, stops and turns as neat and nimble footwork is an absolute requirement for real success. As for your stick, it is important to choose one short enough; a fairly accurate measure is for the top of the handle to reach to your hip joint. Too long a stick will make it impossible for you to properly use the left hand and arm which are the controlling, and sometimes the power factors in performance. It is more to one's advantage to have too short than too long a stick.

THE GRIP

Placing the stick on the ground in front of you, shake hands with the left hand at the top of the stick, spreading your fingers slightly. Place your right hand in a similar position two to four inches below the left. Now face the flat part of your stick forward and if your hands are gripping the stick properly, the back of the left hand and the palm of your right hand will face forward. Lean forward easily from the waist and let your left shoulder be slightly ahead of your right. By doing this it should be possible to make a fairly straight line from your left elbow down to the curve of your stick. This position is important for making sure that your stick is ahead and to the right of your feet and that your head is over the ball as you play it. The stick is usually used in a position perpendicular to the ground or in some circumstances slanted slightly forward from the top of the handle down. It should never be slanted back towards you as the ball can either run up your stick or at least over its blade.

THE DRIBBLE

The ability to carry the ball quickly and with control—that is, being able to run as fast as you can and yet keep the ball always within reach of your stick in order to do next with it what you will, whether it be to pass, to dodge, or to shoot—is a good dribble.

The ball should be carried in front and slightly to the right of your feet, propelled by easy wrist and arm motion making short taps behind the ball, the blade of the stick moving constantly parallel to and close to the ground. Your head should be over the ball yet so you can watch it, the approach of your opponent, and the situation into which you are moving. (Figure 2)

Figure 2

From the beginning, make yourself move as quickly as possible. Dribble with short, quick running steps, then with long strides, then with short quick steps again. Dribble forward; then, keeping the same grip but rotating the face of your stick towards you, run backwards tapping the ball towards you but never letting it catch up to your feet. Run to the left and to the right, bringing the ball with you and always close to your stick. Run forward and then make a quick turn to your right, keeping the ball on your right by twisting well around with the left shoulder leading. The ball should consequently move in a small circle and your feet in a slightly larger one. In the turn your feet will literally be ahead of the ball. In working on this particular move, you could first use long strides and then, without breaking your pace, change into the necessary small quick steps that are needed to bring the ball and yourself around.

Another practice is to roll the ball along the ground ahead of you, run after it at top speed, stick on the ground as you approach, catching up before it stops and bring it into control as you turn quickly to your right with feet and left shoulder leading, and dribble back to place. Dribbling with just the left hand is an excellent practice; keep the stick well away from your feet and close behind the ball.

It is most important to dribble the ball **in front** and slightly to the right of your feet.

THE DRIVE

Any game will bog down if the ball does not or cannot travel for most any distance at any angle at the proper time. Otherwise the challenge to and interest of all players will soon waver and the game will lose its motion and purpose.

For the drive, the principal points to remember are: your hands are together, the left shoulder must point in the direction of the drive, and your head must be over the ball. As your shoulders pivot, the arms should swing back easily, left arm straight and right arm as relaxed as possible, and your wrists should be cocked. (Figure 3) The impact of the stick comes down behind and on through the ball, keeping the stick on the ball as long as possible. The follow-through should be made with arms straight, wrists firm, and the blade of the stick facing upwards. The motion of the body and your weight should flow through in the direction of the hit. Aim for a short back swing, quick hit, and low follow-through. These will prevent "sticks," and also the ability to take a quick hit, thereby disguising your intention until the last moment, will often deceive your opponent.

In order to feel the swing of the stick and the shoulders, try hitting with just the left hand and then with the right hand alone. Then begin running and hitting as one motion, for you should be able to get off a quick hit without changing pace. Always remember to **place your feet in relation to the ball,** depending upon the direction you wish to hit, **not** placing the ball in relation to your feet. The latter makes for slow play, poor stickwork and lazy footwork.

To drive the ball to the left while running, it should be in front of the left foot. To drive the ball to the right, there are two different methods: while running straight, let the ball drop behind off the rear foot; give a strong twist of the shoulders to make the direction accurate and to allow **both** arms to swing for the backswing; keep your head over the ball; and follow through in direction of drive, while your feet

Evaluation Questions

Can you dribble forward, then reverse your stick and pull the ball back towards you without letting it catch up to your feet? Can you do this moving left and then right? Can you do all of these at top speed?

continue their forward motion. (Figure 4) The second way is to take a quick side step around the ball as you take the backswing in order to have the left side of your body, from the foot to the shoulder, moving

Figure 3

Figure 4

in the direction of the pass. To drive the ball straight ahead, as in shooting for a goal, the backswing comes as the left shoulder pivots around into the direction of the hit. Control of the body and the stick, keeping the head steady and over the ball, and keeping the body moving in the same plane throughout are all important.

7

Evalution Questions
FIELDING THE BALL

From the beginning, run and drive at specific objects such as stakes, buckets, tins, the goal posts. Work for speed, smoothness, and accuracy. Never just stand and drive back and forth with someone else for in a game, this occurs in only one situation—when taking a corner hit. This is when a player stands on the goal line, drives the ball quickly and accurately to a teammate who is standing on the edge of the circle, and she in turn stops the ball and then drives hard at the goal. It is true also that you are fairly stationary while taking a "free hit," but then you usually hit into a space or to a player who has moved to get free of an opponent.

FIELDING THE BALL

Some are apt to call it stopping the ball, but we prefer to think of it as catching the ball on your stick. You must first be able to receive the ball before you can do something with it. It must be yours, within reach of your stick, to do with it what you will.

We have here the problem of two rather solid objects coming together: one must give. Apply the same principle as you do when catching a ball. Your hand is ready and waiting. As the ball enters your hands, the degree of its force governs how much you will give through your arm and perhaps through your body. Fielding a hockey ball is somewhat similar to catching a grounder in softball.

Your hands on your stick are slightly apart as when dribbling and your stick must be on the ground. You should wait for the ball with the face of the stick at right angles to the direction from which the ball is approaching. As the ball comes onto the stick, loosen your grip ever so

Diagram A:

FIELDING THE BALL

little, enough to absorb the impact, and bring the stick, with the ball on it, back towards you into either a perpendicular position or with the handle inclined slightly forward. Once again, your head must be over the ball, and your feet in any easy position, but never together. If possible, feet and legs should be in position directly behind the line in which the ball is travelling. (Figures 5, 6)

Figure 5

Figure 6

Have a partner roll the ball to you along the ground, fairly directly at first. Have your stick on the ground. Nothing is more frustrating than to have a ball go under your stick. If it bounces over, you can always blame the ground! Catch the ball on your stick, making as little sound

9

as possible on impact. Practice running forward to receive it, keeping it close to your stick. Move quickly backward and receive the ball in this fashion. Increase the speed and vary the direction.

Then work in pairs, hitting and receiving, not too far apart. Speed yourselves up by saying "receive," "hit." The ball should come onto your stick; then move your feet quickly, slip hands together and hit. Do this in the time it takes to say the two words. As soon as you have hit the ball, get your stick back on the ground, ready to receive the ball again.

The principle of receiving the ball remains the same no matter from which direction it is coming. If it is approaching from your right side, by twisting your shoulders you can face the stick at right angles, give with the ball, and then guide it forward into dribbling or driving position. (Figure 7) If it is coming from behind on your right, still run in the direction you wish to go, twist well around through the waist and shoulders, receive the ball and bring it along with you. (Figure 8)

Figure 7   *Figure 8*

A ball coming from your left side requires still another type of body positioning but the same principles apply. If it is coming hard and fast enough and just ahead of you, have your stick at right angles to its flight but in front of your feet, so that as you receive it, it will already be in position for dribbling or driving. If it is a softer hit, go to meet it with the stick on your left side. Move your feet quickly to the left after receiving the ball so that it will then be in front and to your right.

(Figure 9) For a ball coming from behind on the left, twist the top part of the body around so that your stick will meet the ball at right angles, and then move your feet over into position. (Figure 10) Practice by having your partner roll the ball to you as you are running straight ahead; later from either side and from behind you. Show your partner by where you place your stick on which side you wish to receive the ball. This is called "asking for the ball."

Stand five to ten yards from your partner, and send the ball to her non-stick side. Make the hit possible to receive, yet enough ahead of her so she must move quickly to receive it on her right. With another quick step, she should return the ball to your non-stick side. It is a receive-hit action, and you will move clockwise.

With your partner five or ten yards from you as you run, start at about the fifty yard line. Dribble the ball a yard or so, look at your partner and pass the ball to her so she can receive it without breaking

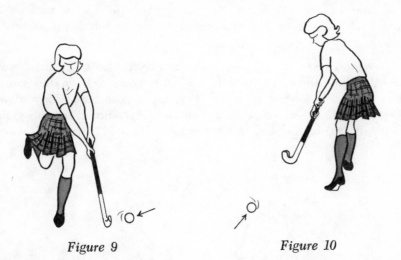

Figure 9   Figure 10

her pace. As soon as you have hit the ball, with a burst of speed catch up to her; she should receive the ball, judge your speed, and pass immediately to you. Work for receive-hit, but also sympathetic passing, trying always to stretch one another into greater speed and quicker footwork. Remember to slide the right hand slightly down the stick when receiving, and back up again for the short, quick pass. Whoever has the ball at the time the edge of the circle is reached should shoot hard and accurately at the goal. As you return up the field, change positions in order to practice hitting and receiving on both sides.

If the ball does not travel as far as you intended, your partner should move in to receive it as you pull away to keep your spacing. In a game it is wise to remember never to follow a pass you have made.

As you practice this passing in twos there is another point to remember which in a game should prove beneficial. If you are the receiver, do not move ahead until your partner makes the pass, even though you must be prepared to do so. This will prevent you from being called offside, should there not be three opponents between you and the goal.

TACKLES

Up to this point, you have been in possession of the ball, but now how does one take the ball from her opponent? We like to think of all tackles as a game of cat and mouse and knowing when to pounce. It could be argued whether the person with the ball or the one about to tackle has the advantage. A player skillful in dodging at top speed welcomes the challenge. However, the player about to pounce matches her timing and can choose her moment of trying to rob her opponent of the ball.

Straight Tackle—As you approach the player who is coming towards you with the ball, move towards her with your stick on the ground. When the ball is farthest from her stick, use a good stride forward with either foot, place your stick in a position perpendicular to the ground or with the top of the stick slightly ahead. (Figure 11) If your timing is

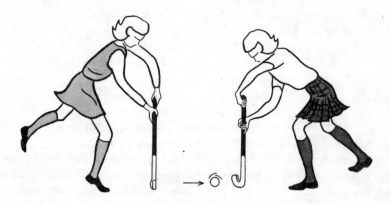

Figure 11

correct, the ball will come onto your stick. At this point, a firm grip is necessary. If the player with the ball is moving rapidly, she will pass right shoulders with you, for in tackling you *play the ball not the person.* If you remember this, you will never bump into an opponent. At the moment of the tackle you should be motionless for two reasons. If you miss the tackle, you can turn rapidly and tackle again (tackle back). How to do that will come later, but it is not too early to learn that if you tackle and miss, you *always tackle back* until either you have possession of the ball or have forced your opponent to pass. The second reason for that instant state of motionlessness is that it will give you the control necessary to pass the ball immediately if you have been successful in gaining its possession. It is practically always true that *as soon as you have made a tackle successfully, pass the ball,* because your opponent who has been robbed will, or should, try to recover it. Reach out for the ball. This will help you to learn how soon you can actually get your stick to the ball and, how soon a dodge must begin.

As you become more skilled, your timing of a straight tackle becomes an even greater challenge. One soon learns what the ball control of an opponent is; if she is a player who can hardly wait for you to tackle, you can move forward, reach and step back, and very often she will dodge into your stick. Of course, your opponent might catch on to this ruse, so you must vary your tactics. It is also true that when opponents are equal in ability, one has only a fifty-fifty chance to perform a successful tackle; but a player who, by tackling, can force an opponent to pass before she is ready is just as successful as if her tackle had come off, provided her teammates are alert and ready to intercept the pass.

Two-handed Tackle from the Left—Assume that the player has passed by you and is on your left and you are running after her. A player without the ball should be able to run faster than the player with the ball. Catch her, keep both hands on your stick, and reach to put your stick just ahead of the ball so that the ball will come onto it. Your opponent should overrun, and you can turn and hit immediately. Once you have mastered the timing of this maneuver, you can proceed to a more difficult one. Instead of placing your stick on the ground, reach in with the toe of your stick and pull the ball quickly from in front of her. (Figure 12) At the same time, pivot your body, stopping with the weight on your right foot so that your left is ready to lead into the drive that should follow. It will take practice to simultaneously coordinate the pull of the ball and the movement of your feet. In the beginning, you may pull the ball too vigorously so that it comes too far to your right; in trying to

Figure 12

retrieve it, it is possible that your body will come between your opponent and the ball as she also tries to recover it. In a game you would then be called for obstruction.

Before going on, it is well to remember that a foul occurs if you hit your opponent's stick if you trip her, or if you impede her progress by pushing her or breaking her stride.

Left Hand Lunge—To be used when you cannot quite catch up to your opponent or when you must try to get the ball sooner than the time it would take to get on a level with her. As the name implies, it is done with the left hand, and you will stretch and lunge from slightly behind. (Figure 13) Being as far to the right of your opponent as your utmost

Figure 13

reach will allow is desirable as it adds an element of surprise. Failure to be well away is a common fault. The stick is controlled by the left hand and arm, but the impetus is given by the right hand. As the stick leaves the right hand, it should move as parallel to the ground as possible and be aimed just ahead of the ball. Utmost control is necessary—the

Evaluation Questions

If your partner dribbles the ball about two feet from your side line, can you do a circular tackle keeping the ball within the boundary?

right hand literally gives the power, the left hand and arm must prevent the stick from swinging on through into the legs or stick of your opponent. If you have mistimed your tackle and missed, then immediately replace your right hand on the stick and try again. Do not dangle your stick in front of your opponent.

When the ball has come onto your stick, the tackle is only half completed. As you hold your stick firmly against the ball, turn as rapidly as you can, replace your right hand on the stick, and now play the ball. As someone once said: "The right hand says to the left hand 'You go first and I'll come as soon as I can.'" If by chance you hit the ball on your lunge but cannot keep it on your stick, you have at least accomplished what is called a "spoil" stroke—you have stopped something from happening. But always try for a tackle so you can *do something with the ball,* in which case you have not only spoiled a move of your opponent's, but you have started an attacking move for your own team.

You will now realize that in the tackles described, your action has made you turn to the left. That is because your opponent has been on your left. There are other tackles to use when the player is on your right, and in executing them you will turn to your right. Always remember that *when you are trying to take the ball from an opponent, if she is on your left, you must turn to your left; similarly, if she is on your right, you must turn to your right.* Once you are aware of this, you will be well on your way to understanding and avoiding obstruction.

Circular Tackle—In the previous tackles, you were either on a level with the player or just slightly behind, but always aiming to get your

Figure 14 (1)

Figure 14 (2)

Figure 14 (3)

stick just ahead of the ball. In this tackle, speed is even more important as you must get ahead of your opponent and on a level with the ball when it is farthest from her stick. As your move begins, your stick should be on the ground, ready to take the ball as you sweep around in front of your opponent without causing her to break her stride. Body movement begins with a turn of the shoulders, the left shoulder leading. Use your shoulders as you would the handle bars of a bike. Your hips follow around, as does the rear wheel of a bike. Your feet must stay to the left of the ball during the entire movement to avoid obstruction. Keeping your head over the ball, strive for a small circle with the ball and a slightly larger one with your feet. (Figure 14-1, 2, 3)

A good beginning practice is to have your opponent dribble the ball down the field about two feet from the outside alley line. Tackle, keeping the ball inside the boundary line, even if your feet go over the line. Forcing yourself to execute the tackle within such a narrow area should make you realize how small the arc the ball must travel. To move in such a small circle demands quick footwork. In a game it is legal to have your feet outside as long as the ball remains within bounds.

There are other tackles you can use when your opponent is on your right, but those will be mentioned later. Strive to be proficient at this tackle. Defense players will soon learn that if they are playing on the left hand side of the field this tackle is necessary, as it takes the ball away from the center of the field. For the same reason, the two handed tackle and the left hand lunge are used more on the right side of the field.

DODGES

How to avoid the player who is approaching, intent upon taking the ball away from you? A good maxim to remember is that, if possible, *a pass to a teammate is the best dodge.*

A dodge is, in a sense, a pass to oneself, very neat and controlled. A forward executes a dodge quite differently from a defense player. Except in a corner situation, a forward should be moving quickly, the ball close to her stick, and she should be able to perform the dodge at top speed. Any forward who slows down as she is about to dodge is easy prey for the defense, as she gives away her intent. On the other hand, a defense player is usually not moving as rapidly as she dodges. If she has intercepted a ball and is in a clear space, she will pass the ball almost immediately, not waiting for an opponent to come and tackle her before passing. More often, she has reached the ball just before her opponent, and as she has not the time to make a quick hit, she will dodge the onrushing foward and then pass.

If your dodge is poorly done so that you have to pursue the ball, your teammate may mistake it for a pass. She will then come to meet it, as she should, and this can lead to crowding and chaos.

Pull to the Left—(Figure 15) Imagine that your opponent is coming toward you and the ball you are dribbling, the face of her stick reaching out ready to tackle. With a sudden movement, face your stick directly left and pull the ball in that direction. At the same time, step to the left in order to keep the ball on your right and in the proper position for your next move. These actions should be simultaneous and of just enough scope to avoid your opponent's stick. The action could almost be described as a right angle move by the player, her stick and the ball. For the defense player, a slightly diagonal pull back to the left with a similar step is an even better pattern to work towards and more likely to avoid the oncoming stick of an opponent. Although a forward should also practice this, it would be greatly to her advantage to practice on the run. Her movement will not be so much a pull as a swerve to the left, making the motion almost a semicircle as she sweeps out and around her opponent. (Figure 16) The stick should be kept very close to the ball and her speed should increase as she does the dodge. She should remember to pull around with her left shoulder leading, which will not only help her to move the ball and keep it on the right but also will help avoid obstruction.

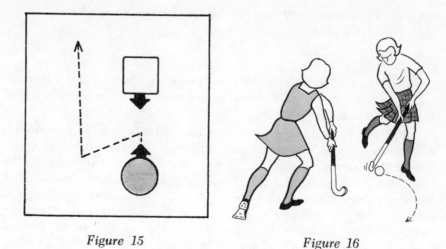

Figure 15   *Figure 16*

To practice any dodge, your opponent must pretend she does not know what you are going to do and move in for a straight on tackle. After you have learned several dodges, she can use any tactics she chooses and you can try to outwit her. If you are practicing as a *forward*, work either near the circle so that you can shoot immediately upon evading your opponent or have an object set up towards which you can shoot or a teammate to whom you can immediately pass. If practicing dodging as a *defense player*, limit your time and space. An excellent practice is to face your opponent with the width of the alley between you. Have your opponent hit a sharp quick hit to you and immediately move towards you with her stick on the ground, trying for a straight on tackle. You must be able to receive the ball and dodge before the tackle is made. If you are successful, take the ball to the opposite alley line, turn to your right, and reverse the procedure by hitting to your opponent and following in for a tackle. This is a small space in which you must act and react, but in a game such a short span of space and time is common. Another practice is to place a ball just in front of a tin or bucket. Stand some ten feet from it, run at top speed towards it, pull the ball gently to the left as you step left, then either dribble or drive at an object.

Dodge to the Non-Stick Side—(Figure 17) Once again, your opponent is coming directly towards your stick. Just before she comes within reach of the ball, push it in a slightly diagonal direction to her non-stick, or left, side. As the ball leaves your stick, you should swerve to your left, dart around her, and pick up the ball again. (Figure 18) Your speed must increase as you go around your opponent in order to meet the ball

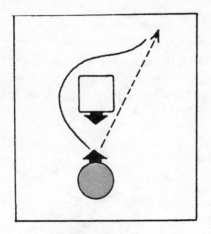

Figure 17

Figure 18

before she can turn to tackle back. Do not push the ball into her feet but angle its path, and do not push or hit it too far ahead. Remember it is a pass to yourself, and you want to be sure you receive it. The importance of moving around your opponent cannot be overstressed. She has already established her position and lack of thought on your part, as well as lack of quick footwork, will cause you to run into her. This leads to roughness and a foul could be called on you. Hockey is not basically a rough game, but poor judgment, poor footwork and poor ball control, plus lack of consideration, can make it so.

Reverse Stick Dodge—(Figure 19) This is a variation of the previous dodge. As your opponent approaches, reverse your stick, pull the ball directly to your right and hit to a teammate. This must be done well before your opponent can reach the ball to avoid the possibility of obstructing her.

The Scoop—The ball must be slightly farther ahead of you than it is in the other dodges, because you must be able to lay the blade of the stick slightly back, enough to lift the ball over your opponent's stick. If the blade is open too far, the ball will roll over the back of it; if not open enough,

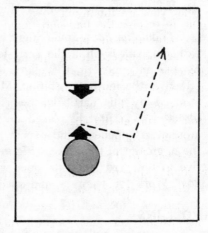

Figure 19

nothing at all will happen. You will be more successful, perhaps, if you slide the right hand a little farther down the stick.

Learn to keep the ball low as it is then harder to intercept. The higher it is the easier it is for your opponent to put her stick to it. Or she may be able to catch the ball in her hand which is a perfectly legal

Figure 20

action as long as she drops it immediately and perpendicularly to the ground. Your scoop should not travel too far, as you want to retrieve it yourself. With this dodge more than with any other, unless it is well done, you will give away through the position of your body or stick what you are intending to do.

Triangular Pass—Some might call it a give-and-take pass. As mentioned earlier a pass is often the best dodge, and certainly a triangular pass to by-pass an opponent, if well timed and well executed, will be the most effective, the most devastating. More space is covered and greater speed attained by this particular maneuver. It is a combination of a flat or direct pass accurately placed onto a teammate's stick, a burst of speed around an opponent, and a neat, diagonal pass ahead by the receiver to the originator of the move. (Figure 21) Practice this dodge with a partner, five to ten yards to your side, with an opponent between you and the goal. Work for accuracy and speed.

ROLL-INS

When the ball goes over the side line off the stick of a player, it is put into play by a member of the opposing team by a roll-in or, as

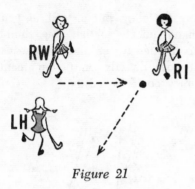

Figure 21

some call it, a roll on. It is usually done by a halfback. Practice rolling the ball with both the left and right hand, keeping your stick in the opposite hand, and releasing the ball along the ground so that it travels smoothly and accurately. The choice of hand depends upon the side of the field on which you are playing. The ball must touch the ground three feet from where it crossed the side line.

The backswing and follow-through of your arm will make or break the accuracy of your roll-in. Start with your partner, you on one side of a line and she on the other, some distance away. Be sure that neither your stick nor your feet are on or over the line as you roll the ball. Swing your arm back and as it swings forward, take a long step forward with the opposite foot. (Figure 22) This lunge will take you low enough

Figure 22

so that your fingers can brush the ground as you release the ball just inside the line along which you are standing. You will already have compared this action with bowling and rightly so. Aim to have the ball travel parallel to and close to the line. Your partner should receive it. Since she is on the other side of the line, she will use the opposite hand and foot when she rolls it back to you. Shift positions so that you both become proficient with either hand.

In any game, you try to outwit and out-think your opponents; subterfuge is exciting. There is a variation of the regular roll-in which is sometimes useful and effective. With a good backswing and step, pretend that you are going to make a long roll up the alley, but instead, as your arm swings down by you, rotate your hand quickly so that your thumb is towards the ground, and release the ball sideways or diagonally backwards. (Figure 23) Make sure that it goes directly onto your teammate's stick as, in a game, lack of accuracy could be costly.

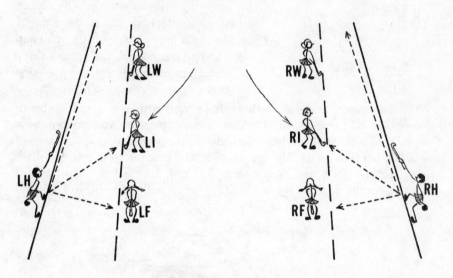

Figure 23

THE BULLY

This is the means by which the game is started at the beginning of each half; after each goal is scored; when the ball goes over the goal line or the side line off the sticks of two opponents simultaneously; ~~or when a penalty bully is awarded~~. As this latter term sounds rather awesome, it should be explained now. If any defense player commits a foul when, in the opinion of the umpire, a goal most likely would otherwise have been scored, the defense player concerned and any member of the opposing team take a ~~bully five~~ PENALTY STROKE SEVEN yards in front of the goal. All other players of the two teams stand and wait beyond the 25-yard line. The fouls the defense player might have committed are using the wrong side of her stick; making sticks; obstruction; advancing the ball; or using her feet (unless she is the goalkeeper). Because there is always the possibility of such a situation all players should know how to bully.

In all bullies, place the ball on a line between you and your opponent. This line may be an imaginary one as in the case of a 25-yard line bully, a wing bully, or a penalty bully. Each of you must stand with your feet parallel astride the line and not very far apart. Your weight should be on the balls of your feet, your head over the ball, your right hand a little farther down your stick than usual, and the blade of your stick on the ground close behind the ball. You and your opponent now lift your sticks and touch them just over the ball, and replace them again behind the ball. A bully is completed when you have hit the ground and your opponent's stick three times. You may move your feet only on completion of the bully and, as quickness is important at this point, this explains the purpose of keeping your feet fairly close together and your weight forward. Work for speed on the "ground-sticks," and at the same time keep your stick as close to the ball as possible without actually touching it. If the ball is touched, the bully must be repeated.

Once the bully is completed, you must attempt to gain possession of the ball rapidly and get it to one of your teammates. This can be accomplished in several different ways.

1. Place your stick on the ball and pull it rapidly towards you, making your feet move backward at the same time, and make a sharp quick hit to your left. Remember that you cannot turn your shoulder or your body on your opponent, hence the quick and simultaneous movement directly backwards.

2. Draw the ball diagonally backwards, moving your right foot at the same time, and hit to the right.

3. Reverse your stick and, with its toe, send the ball back to your teammate who is backing up the bully five yards from you.

4. Quickly lift your stick up as your opponent brings her stick onto the ball, and the ball will go to your teammate.

5. If your opponent's stick and yours are deadlocked against the ball, a firm forward and upward movement of your stick could lift the ball up and over her stick; then follow with a quick pass.

The forwards will move across the line at the third hit of sticks ready for the ball. (In the case of the penalty bully, since you will have no teammate to whom to pass, you should try to shoot immediately if you are a forward, and try to clear the ball out of the circle if you are a defense player.)

3

Playing the Game - Positions

GENERAL POINTS FOR ALL PLAYERS TO REMEMBER

1. Keep two hands on your stick at all times unless you need the added reach which is only possible with one hand. This latter effort presumes, of course, that you are not just lazy with your feet.

2. Hold your stick near or on the ground at all times. Place it on the ground whenever there is a possibility that you are about to play the ball. A "carpet sweeper" action is ideal!

3. Move to meet a pass or to intercept a pass.

4. Be constantly aware of spacing of your own team and of your opponents.

5. Never have any more than two players on the ball at any one time. Give these two an opportunity to accomplish what each is attempting and space in which to do it, but always be prepared for the next play.

6. Know your opponent! Try to learn as soon as possible her strengths and weaknesses. Above all, remember that if someone other than your immediate opponent is attempting to take the ball from you, most likely someone on your team is free. Find her and use her. Following are some examples:

   (a) You are an inner and the center-half tries to take the ball from you. Send the ball to the center-forward.

   (b) You are a wing halfback and your opposing wing halfback comes in to tackle; get the ball to your wing.

(c) You are a wing and you have passed your opposing halfback and the fullback moves in on you; immediately pass to the inner.

7. Always tackle back, even if you think there is no chance to recover the ball. Being hurried can be frustrating to your opponent.

8. Be constantly on the move both mentally and physically because the ball can travel at great speed and for great distances. Each time the ball is hit, the angles change by which it can next travel.

9. Whether you are a forward or a defense player, remember to *use your wings*. They are so often neglected, and they can be used to great advantage, no matter in which part of the field the ball is being played. By using the wings and spreading the play, your opposing defense is also spread out, thereby creating spaces into which your own forwards may move and receive passes.

10. Never hit the ball back to the place from which it came since there must be an opponent there. Look up, find the best opening and then change the direction of the play.

11. Avoid "hit and hope" passes—hitting just to get rid of the ball and hoping your opponents will miss it. This occurs mainly when a team is hard pressed.

FORWARD PLAY

The ultimate purpose of the forward line players is to score goals, and the effort to accomplish this must be relentless. The challenge for you and your four teammates should be a constant one of trying to outwit and to outmaneuver your opposing defense. There is always the choice for you, through speed and ball control, to score on sheer individual play, and this should be done whenever the opportunity arises; but more often the scoring of goals is the combination of five forwards thinking as one. Alertness, ball control, and anticipation, combined with footwork, stickwork, and determination, are the ultimate aims for which you must strive.

Whether the ball is in the attacking or the defending end of the field, there is work for you to do. Constantly positioning yourself in relation to your teammates and your opponents so that you are free to receive a pass will make you not only a contributing forward but also a scoring one.

The defense must operate on basic principles in order to prevent chaos! To be an effective forward you should understand them because your moves must be to upset and outplay the marking and covering of

Can you name several reasons why forwards should attempt to stay in line with one another when one of them has the ball?

Evalution Questions

the defense. A forward should be crafty, foxy, and unpredictable in her moves, quick off the mark, not afraid to be an individual, one who uses the basis of the defense to set up the play against them and to take quick advantage of any mistake made by them.

You should learn to bully well and to make corners count. The latter means being able to hit the ball hard and accurately to the player who is to receive it, and she in turn must have the ability to field the ball close to her stick and shoot immediately for goal. Moving and making yourself available to receive a free hit or roll-in, or marking an opponent when the free hit or roll-in is awarded against your team are other musts for you as a forward.

As your season progresses and players have made their choice between forward and defense positions, at some time forwards and defense players should change places with one another. Only in this way will you learn what to expect from one another. Each position on the field has both similar and different problems and your ability to understand them will make for greater effectiveness in relation to the team as a whole.

GENERAL AND BASIC PRINCIPLES FOR ALL FORWARDS

1. Move across the line immediately after the bully, ready to receive a pass and to open the space between you and your own defense.
2. Each forward has approximately 12 yards in which to move laterally. This is not to say that a forward cannot move out of this imaginary lane, but it should emphasize the spacing which is desirable. Maintaining such spacing increases the difficulty of marking and covering for defense players.

3. Never be so close to another forward that one defense player can be responsible for both. This will defeat any move, as you have in essence given your opponents an extra defender.

4. Always receive the ball with your feet facing in the direction of the goal you are attacking.

5. Never follow a pass you have made. If you pull away, you will give your teammate space into which to move to receive the pass. At the same time you will either draw your opposing defense away from the receiver or you will be free to receive a return pass.

6. In your attacking end of the field be constantly aware of your opposing defense and where they are. Why?

(a) Offside. If you are ahead of the ball when it is hit and there are not three defense players between you and the goal, a foul may be called. A player who is offside can spoil an attacking movement and be provoking to her teammates. If one of your teammates has the ball, and there are not the necessary three defense players between her and the goal, move on a line with her, staying one step behind the ball. If then your teammate decides to pass to you, either directly or ahead into a space, you cannot be called for offside when you move ahead to play the ball. It would be well to remember always that *in your attacking half of the field, if you will stay on a line with the forward who has the ball, regardless of the defense, being offside will be no problem.* Anticipate the pass that might come, and then move ahead with a burst of speed to receive it.

(b) A forward line which is not a line is more easily covered by a defense, for a defense player can then not only mark you but cover the space as well. (Figures 24, 25)

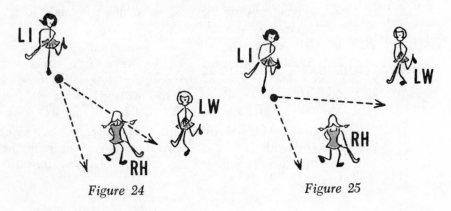

Figure 24   Figure 25

7. Interchange of positions by forwards is effective if it does not become a constant pattern, and if the other forwards are quick to adjust to the spacing. Dictated by the situation, it can, for the moment, be chaotic for the defense. If done too much, its effect on the defense is lessened and thereby loses its purpose. If interchange does take place, do not shift back too soon—wait until the situation which caused the original move has passed. Helter skelter rushing back and forth may confuse your own team more than your opponents.

8. It is possible and wise and deceptive at times to disguise your pass by dribbling slightly in one direction to draw your opponent and then pass in the opposite direction.

9. *In the circle:*

   (a) Keep moving in relation to the ball. A forward who remains stationary, or almost so, as a teammate plays the ball is a delight to play against. Her opposing defense can then concentrate on just her own positioning in relation to the ball. On the contrary, a forward who constantly shifts, moving forward, backward, or sideways, ready to pounce and shoot, can make life quite miserable for her opponent who must watch both player and ball.

   (b) Know where the goal is in relation to the ball so that you will be prepared to rush a shot for goal or will not miss the goal on your try for it.

   (c) Never assume that the ball is going into the goal or that the goalkeeper will miss it. Every effort must be made to get your stick on the ball and put it over the goal line. Similarly, try to stop any ball from going over the end line, not between the goal posts, and keep it in play for still another chance to score.

   (d) The three inside forwards in general do the shooting and rushing, each moving toward the goal at a different angle to try to cover the clears of the goalie.

   (e) Though the forward who takes the initial shot for the goal must rush, her fellow forwards should move with the backswing of the initial shot in order to arrive in time to get the rebound from the goalkeeper's pads, if she has managed the save. Most goals are not scored from the initial shot but by the follow-up.

   (f) If either of the wings sends a pass straight across the circle, move forward with your stick down and "sweep" or push the ball into the goal. If either wing shoots, the inside forwards should rush.

(g) If the ball is cleared out behind you in the circle and one of your halfbacks is about to shoot, make a space for her to shoot and then follow in the shot.

(h) If the circle seems crowded, it is often the fault of the forwards who have bunched together. A defense player must follow her forward, so try to keep spaces. If the defense player does not move with you, then you are free. If she does move, there is a space for the ball and you to move into.

(i) You, as a forward, have a tremendous advantage in the circle, as you are facing the goal and can continually move on to the ball, whereas the defender has her back to the goal. A ball that goes behind a defense player should therefore be moved upon immediately and with great advantage since the defender must first turn herself about in order to tackle.

In the Defending Half of the Field

(a) If your opponents capture the ball and start down the field, never stop moving until you have crossed over the 50-yard line. How much farther back you move depends on how hard pressed your defense is and where the ball is.

(b) Your defense should be able to clear the ball to you and you should expect them to do so. However, you must be moving and showing by the position of your stick where you want the ball. If you are being closely marked, by moving you can draw your defense with you and make a space through which your teammate can pass the ball. If the space is covered by your opponent, then you are free to ask for the ball.

(c) When a defense is having difficulty clearing the ball to its attack, the forwards on that side of the field should drop back in order to tackle back on the players who are intercepting the ball.

(d) There are many systems for forwards to use in the defending half of the field, particularly when the ball is in the defending circle or near it. One is called the W formation, in which the wings remain up near the center line, as does the center forward, while the two inners drop back to help the defense. If either inner gets the ball she passes it ahead to a wing or to the center forward and then both inners recover and catch up with the rest of the line. Another formation, the reverse, could be called the M formation: the center forward and wings are back and the inners are well up the field. A third is when the forwards on the side the ball is on are back, and the forwards on the other side are ahead, ready to receive. As the situation constantly changes in the circle, these formations must be very fluid and cannot be preplanned.

WINGS—GENERAL. A wing must be always available, whether on the attack or on the defense. Except on a roll-in when it is impossible, play with your back towards the side line as you move up and down the field asking for the ball. In this way you can always be aware of the position of the ball, of your teammates and of your opponents.

Wings must be able to pass or hit at will with the proper speed and direction. A drive to your opposite wing or inner is most effective to both vary the play and make your defense shift. If you can pass the ball as the defense is shifting and before they are ready to tackle or intercept, do so. A defense which is running back to recover can sometimes be caught off balance, very often facing in the wrong direction.

Remember to drop back towards your own halfback or fullback who is taking a free hit if there is no space through which she can send the ball ahead. You are then available for a direct pass, or you will have drawn your opposing halfback, thereby opening up a space for your teammate's pass. (Figures 26, 27)

If you can dribble the ball in or close to the side line it will be much more difficult for your opponent to try to take the ball without going over the side line.

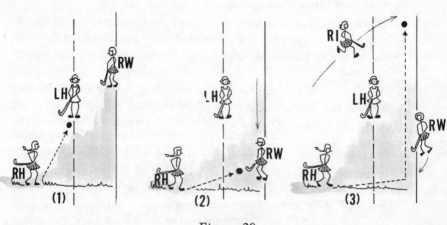

Figure 26

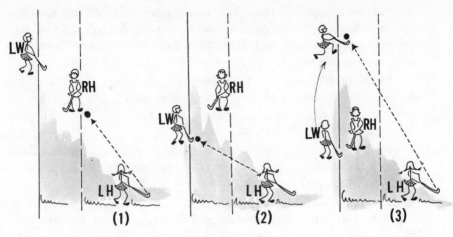

Figure 27

If you have possession of the ball and are free between the 25-yard line and the circle, start to cut in towards the circle and get your shot away immediately upon reaching the edge of the circle.

Once you have passed your opponent, vary your moves; for example:

1. If you have dodged her, you should sometimes pass immediately.
2. Any halfback who has been passed will try to tackle back; listen for her approach and pass before she tackles.
3. Once a halfback is passed, you can sometimes lure a fullback to come and try her luck, but be sure to pass in time to the inner who is free since you have drawn her fullback.
4. A wing who has passed her halfback and who cannot lure her fullback, and still continues to carry the ball until her opposing defense has an opportunity to get back to intercept the pass that must eventually come, has thrown away a golden opportunity. Try instead to catch your defense in the act of shifting. Of course if you are ahead of your forward line, you must continue your solo run.

Wings should practice over and over again taking corner hits and making their drives hard, accurate and smooth. They also should learn to do a strong push pass as a variation of the hit in a corner situation, for on some grounds this is easier for the forwards to receive.

LEFT WING

1. Position yourself on the outside alley line or even over it if you wish. By taking advantage of the full width of the field, you will make the

task of your opposing right half much more difficult. Because her non-stick is toward the center as she faces you, she will have to play further in and back so as not to allow the ball to be put through to you on that side.

2. As the right half must play slightly in and deeper, left wings are often guilty of moving ahead too soon, thus either getting offside or making it impossible to receive the pass. Keep on a line with your other forwards if they have the ball.

3. If your own halfback or fullback has the ball, and your opposing halfback is covering the space rather than marking you, be prepared to drop well back and out, ready to receive the ball.

4. Constant practice of your drives to the right, striving to pass or to hit at will with the proper speed and direction is very important.

5. On a roll-in you are more easily marked than a right wing since the alley is on the stick side of your opposing halfback. If she is marking closely and you want the ball rolled in well up the field along the outside line, then move back towards your own halfback who is taking the roll-in. If your opposing halfback moves back with you, you can then be on your way with the roll, and your opposing half will have to turn and chase. If your halfback decides to roll the ball to your own inner or fullback, immediately *pull well out to the side line,* with your back to it, prepared for the pass which is inevitable because: (a) whenever a forward receives a ball or gets it behind her own forward line, she should always pass ahead to one of the other forwards and then catch up to the line; (b) a defense player will always pass the ball as soon as she can in order to get her team on to the attack.

6. As you become more skilled, practice using a reverse stick for two reasons: (a) even though you are running as fast as you can, a pass may be too far ahead to receive on your right side. Be able to reverse your stick and reach out with either both hands on your stick or, if necessary, only the left, to prevent the ball from going over the side line. (b) a reverse stick drive is difficult but a very necesary part of your playing vocabulary. There will come moments when the ball is near the end or the side line, and it would take too long for your feet to catch up in order to take the right drive. This is an instance when a reverse stick drive either straight across or diagonally back will prove invaluable. It must be done before your opponent is within reach of the ball to avoid obstruction.

RIGHT WING

1. On rolls-in, your opposing halfback will be at a disadvantage as the side line will be on her non-stick side. Usually the best roll-in for your own halfback is straight down the side line. In order to make this effective, do not position yourself too far ahead of your own halfback as your opposing half will have an equal opportunity to move into the alley and get to the ball. Be on your way as the ball leaves her hand, ready to rush by your opponent and catch up with the ball.

   If on the above roll your opposing halfback is protecting her non-stick side by placing herself further from you, then your own halfback should consider rolling the ball directly to you. If this happens, you should pass immediately or place it past your opposing halfback on her non-stick side. Your inner can then dash ahead to get it and you can immediately interchange into the inner's position.

2. If you have the ball near the end line, and a pass across would take the ball to your opposing defense, send it diagonally backwards to any of your inside forwards or to your halfbacks who should be backing up the line. These receivers should be able to get a shot away for the goal.

3. Be prepared for passes much further ahead of you than if you were playing left wing.

INNERS—GENERAL

1. Though goals should be scored by all forwards, they are more often made by inners because of the position they occupy on the forward line. The opportunities for wings to shoot are fewer because of their angle to the goal mouth; they are more fetchers and carriers. A center forward can be effectively bottled up by a competent center-half whose only task as a defense player is to insure that her opposing center forward never gets the ball. Inners, on the other hand, are marked by the fullbacks who must never be on a level with one another. One fullback is up, on the side where the play is, and the other is back, covering for the long through pass. You are the players who can dart in and out and back and forth. You are the players who will do most of the rushing to follow up shots for goal. Each of you will do this at different angles, going in diagonally to cover the more usual clears or rebounds from the goalkeeper. Just as the wings usually take the corner hits, inners usually receive the ball and shoot for goal.

2. Be sure to know if you are suddenly being marked or tackled by the opposing halfback instead of your fullback. If this happens, pass to your wing immediately. She is free.

3. When your opponents have a free hit, mark your opposing inner quickly. This leaves your fullback free to cover the spaces.

4. When your own team has a roll-in, move back and to the inside alley line quickly, before you can be marked by your opposing inner or fullback, thereby giving your halfback another choice for rolling the ball. If you receive it, send it on ahead to your wing or across the field to another forward. Do not keep it, as you are now behind your own forward line.

5. Be prepared to mark your opposing inner on a roll-in.

6. Practice bullies—competency here gives a great advantage to your team.

7. When your defense is hard pressed in and near the circle, be prepared to drop back to receive a pass or to tackle back on the forward who has intercepted the pass from your defense. If you get the ball, get it to one of your teammates immediately and then catch up.

8. Be prepared to run to meet all passes meant for you. Do not wait for the ball to come to you.

9. Be able to dodge at top speed. Also be able to do a quick dodge and shot from the edge of the circle. You will often be rushed on a corner by your opposing halfback or fullback, and if you are unable to get your shot away immediately, a dodge and then a shot can be devastating.

10. In your opponents' circle keep moving constantly, thereby dividing the attention of your opposing fullbacks, who must not only stay within stick's reach of you, but must constantly shift in relation to the ball. If the ball is cleared behind you either move back quickly to try to get it or at least be prepared to move in again on the attack as one of your teammates shoots.

11. It is just as important for you as it is for wings to be able to drive a ball across the field to your opposite inner or wing.

RIGHT INNER. Although passes to you are perhaps more easily intercepted when they come from your left, if you are quick to move to meet them your position makes it somewhat easier to pass, to shoot, and to rush. Fleetness of foot when receiving a ball from your right can carry you by the non-stick side of that stalking left fullback.

Your passes to your right wing can be well ahead because of the very nature of her position and the reach of her stick.

On receiving a corner hit, your feet are already in position to shoot quickly. Just make sure your left shoulder points towards the goal. A dodge to the non-stick side of your opponent as she rushes out to you should be a very particular part of your hockey vocabulary for use on a corner.

LEFT INNER. You will receive most of your passes from your right. With your feet well to the left of your stick and with the necessary twist of your shoulders, you will almost be facing the ball as it comes to you. Go to meet any pass from the right side, as with speed you can take it through to the non-stick side of your opposing defense.

Your left wing should use you often for a pass to avoid her halfback, and you should be prepared not only for this but ready to pass the ball on ahead to her immediately. Teamwork with your wing can be devastating to the opposing right half when you use a triangular pass to get by or through the defense, and it is the ultimate of perfection in forward play.

You will be used often to receive corner hits as it is more difficult for opposing defense to come out on your stick side. Also, you have the perfect angle for shooting to the non-stick side of the goalkeeper. Use the left dodge not only at corners but any time, for your opposing right fullback will most often approach you on an angle to protect her non-stick side.

CENTER FORWARD. Because the opposing center-half has you as her sole opponent, you will very often feel hemmed in. If, however, you continually position yourself in relation to the ball, you will constantly worry her and she will be unable to leave you alone for a second. If, on the other hand, she is one of those roving center halves easily tempted into tackling an inner, move to get free in order to be used by that inner for a pass.

Strive to become successful on your bullies. A center forward who can get the ball immediately into the attack, and preferably through to her wing, is a boon indeed to her team.

Whenever your opposing center-half intercepts a pass to you, give her hot pursuit until either you get the ball or she gets rid of it.

If your opposing half is a threat because she constantly shoots for the goal, it is your job to try to prevent her not only by being aware of her potential danger but by tackling. A center forward who only "stands and waits" will be a detriment to her team.

Which tackle has been attempted
here? Having missed the ball,
what should the tackler do next?

Evolution Questions
TACKLING

A center forward must have space in which to move and her inners must give her this, but at the same time you in your desire to make a space must not crowd the inners.

In the circle be prepared to shoot and to rush. Practice receiving hits on corners.

Defense Play—To play against a skillful and fast forward line is an exciting challenge, exhilarating and exhausting. A defense which understands the demands of each position, which does not panic under pressure, which is sympathetic to each situation as it occurs, and which is capable of both anticipation and concentration, is the ultimate aim of any team.

The old adage is true that "the best defense is a good offense." Every member of the defense must be aware that it is possible for her to start an attack. No player should be satisfied with merely preventing her opponent from scoring.

As a member of the defense, your main purpose is continually to place yourself in such a way that you are prepared to intercept any pass meant for your opponent. This requires constant moving in relation to the ball and to the path it could travel to her, and being on what is commonly called the ball side of your opponent. If you should miss this interception, be prepared to tackle immediately. If you are successful in getting control of the ball, pass it at once to one of your forwards; if you are not successful, continue to pursue your opponent until you are successful or have forced her to pass it.

Work on the accuracy and distance of your drives and the ability to hit to the left or the right with equal success so you can send the ball

Diagram B:
TACKLING

wherever you see a space and a forward ready for it. Accuracy is important because you must avoid the opposing defense which is placing itself to intercept; distance and direction are important because a good forward line will have distance between them and their own defense, and will only move back closer to you if you are hard pressed in or near your defending circle. Forwards expect their defense to be able to get the ball up to them. They constantly maneuver themselves and their opponents to make a space through which the ball may travel, or move in such a way that you can literally "put the ball" on their sticks.

Rarely does one hit the ball straight ahead, as usually an opposing defender will be ready to take it before your teammate can.

When in the circle or moving in to intercept a pass or execute a tackle, always KEEP YOUR STICK ON THE GROUND. Too often a player is either beautifully positioned for an interception, or moves in with great stealth to do a tackle, and the ball goes under her stick because she forgot this most basic point. Avoid this frustrating and maddening experience. The ball does travel on the ground nine times out of ten!

Another important point to remember is that when you go in for a straight on tackle, your stick must be slightly to the right and in front of your feet so you will be in position to play the ball and the stick of your opponent. This is not only good hockey but it is also safer! If you miss on the tackle, you will at least pass by her and not bump into her, and if she decides to shoot or pass, your legs will not be directly behind

37

your stick. This is particularly true as you are rushing out at a corner. A forward must shoot and shoot hard; come out stick to stick and not head to head or legs to legs.

As a defense player, never hit a ball that is coming towards you back in the opposite direction without first controlling it. Hitting the ball on the fly causes it to rise, and dangerous hitting will be called by the official. This is one reason why, on a corner, the rules stipulate that the forward receiving the hit must first control the ball before shooting.

A defense player almost never dribbles the ball, at least for any distance; her main purpose is to get it to her forwards. If she must dodge an opponent before she can pass, she does; otherwise she controls the ball and passes immediately.

As the play comes down the opposite side of the field, increase your speed well ahead of the onrushing forwards in order to be in position and turned around with your back to your goal line, so that you are ready. Any defense player facing the goal line she is defending as she plays the ball is in desperate trouble, both from the point of view of fouling and of trying to clear the ball. You should never clear without first looking to see where to send the ball.

HALFBACKS—GENERAL. Why the name halfbacks? Well, in all truth, they are also half forwards. A good halfback is one who also shoots goals. Halfbacks are *all* defense as well as *half* forwards, so it is understandable that playing half, particularly a wing half, is the most energetic position on the field and one that combines all the facets of the game. To be on the edge of your opponents' circle one moment, either backing up your forwards or trying to shoot; the next moment to be back in your own circle defending; to mark the wing if the ball is on your side of the field, or the inner if the ball is on the other side—take stamina, superb concentration, and anticipation. Its reward is that never are you not in every move of the game.

As your own forwards move down the field with the ball, you are behind them, cognizant that your own opponent is now behind you. If the opposing defense secures the ball you must try to cover any space through which it might travel to your opponent, attempting to intercept it and give it back to your own forwards. If the ball does get by you to your opponent, recover quickly and tackle. If the ball is cleared down the other side of the field, you must still turn and go back to cover the space where the ball might come through to your immediate opponent.

Left and right halfbacks will vary in their positioning because of stick and non-stick sides. You should mark your opponent or cover a space with this thought constantly in mind!

If you are truly attacking halfbacks, the defense will feel the strength and power not of just five forwards but of eight people who are determined to make goals. As a defending halfback, when you are faced with the predicament of such a formidable attack, you will more fully appreciate the coordination and principles of a sound defense.

As halfbacks, particularly wing halves, be prepared to assist your fullback when she is taking a free hit. When a fullback, especially between her own 25-yard line and the circle, is unable to find either a space or a forward free to receive a free hit, you can quickly drop back on a level with her. The fullback should be alert to your offer to help and she should "put the ball" onto your stick and, if done quickly, a space should be available through which you can pass the ball.

In your attacking circle, be prepared to stop any clears and either try for a goal yourself or pass to one of your teammates who may be in a better position. Be ready also for any pass backwards from either your inners or wings, for this is a command for you to shoot and they are prepared to follow up your shot.

As your forwards move up the field with the ball, follow them or back them up. (This does not mean you should climb up their heels.) If an opposing half gets the ball, do not be tempted to tackle *unless* you are sure of retrieving it. If you tackle and miss, your opponent is *free*. It is generally a good policy to let your teammate tackle back on the opponent, rather than rushing in to help. You should give her space in which to maneuver, being prepared, if your opposing defense player retains the ball, to intercept the pass. Players trying to get the ball from one another need space to tackle and tackle again. All too often one sees three people on the ball. Three is a crowd, and someone is wrong. Try never to be that person!

LEFT HALFBACK. Practice all tackles from the left and for this you need speed: the circular tackle, the jab, the right hand lunge. Although tackling on the left side of the field is more difficult, it is easier to cover a space and to clear the ball because of your stick side.

When the ball is on the other side of the field, your left fullback is in a covering position. If your opponents have the ball, you therefore should move in toward the receiving side of the opposing inner to prevent a pass coming through to her. (Your opposing wing, being farthest from the ball, is at the moment less dangerous.) If you are successful in intercepting a pass, send the ball immediately to your forwards. If you are unsuccessful, move back onto your wing at once. You can now disregard the inner as your fullback will move in to take her as soon as she can.

As a left half you can and must be of great assistance to both your goalkeeper and your left fullback in the circle. If neither has the opportunity to make a clear, you may be the initial target for the defensive clear, so be prepared at all times to receive the ball and start it on its way down the field.

Rolls-in are taken with your right hand. The direction is governed by the fact that a right half has an easier time marking her opposing wing than you do. Have a working arrangement with your left wing as to when she should move back towards you in her attempt to draw her opposing halfback with her. If your wing is successful in drawing the halfback, then roll the ball well down the outside alley line. If the halfback is not drawn, roll it on to your wing's stick. You also have the opportunity to use your own inner or fullback. Should you use either, be prepared for them to tap the ball back on to your stick for, if it is impossible for them to find a space through which to send a right drive to the other side of the field, you could then give the ball a good cracking hit down the alley for a quick wing or inner to catch up with. Do not use your fullback for a roll-in between your 25-yard line and the end line.

RIGHT HALFBACK. To protect your non-stick side, you will play slightly farther in on the field when marking your wing or covering the space than the left halfback. Although it is easier to tackle when you play on the right, it is more difficult to cover or clear the ball. This is particularly true in or near the circle, as you do not want to clear across your goal or block the view (unsight) of your goalkeeper.

As you come out on corner hits, be sure to get your feet well to the left and not directly behind your stick. You must be quick of foot.

Your rolls-in must be done with your left hand. Keep in mind that the left halfback against you has a more difficult task of marking your right wing on the roll-in because your side line is on her non-stick side. Your most usual roll therefore should be as close as possible to the outside line. Of course you may also use your inner and fullback. As a change of pace and as a surprise tactic, *and if your fullback is prepared and ready,* feint a long roll down the alley, then quickly reverse your hand and send the ball only a foot or two into the alley directly towards your fullback. She should immediately step towards it; she has the choice of driving it across the field, down the alley close to the side line, or to her inner. It would be unwise to use this roll-in behind the 25-yard line.

CENTER-HALF. Although all players should be able to hit both to the left and to the right, the center-half is responsible for distributing the play. Often one side of a field will become quite exhausted, while the other half eagerly awaits action and then becomes bored. You are the pivot around whom the rest of the defense moves. The stability of any defense hangs upon your ability to be concerned only with your opposing center forward. If you are easily tempted by an inner who has the ball and you leave your center forward free, the breakdown of the defense begins. Of course if an opposing inner is so close to her center forward that you can reach and tackle her without actually leaving the center forward, do so. In good hockey even this won't work, however, for an intelligent center forward will quickly pull away and be free of you. Your task is never to let this happen.

As your opponents swing the ball from one side of the field to the other, move to place yourself between your opposing center forward and the ball, moving left or right to what is commonly known as the receiving, or ball side, of your opponent.

In your defending circle, mark closely. Never leave your opponent free. If by chance the left inner or opposing center-half is on your right, about to shoot and free to do so, a quick lunge without leaving your opponent is necessary. If your opposing center-half comes through on your left to shoot, your left fullback will spoil the shot if possible, as the player is on her stick side.

FULLBACKS—GENERAL. Your opponent is the inner and your main objective is to keep her from scoring. Remember that you and your other fullback must never be on a level with one another, except when you are in the circle defending. As you and your team become more proficient, even this exception can be eliminated. This more advanced level of play will be described later. At the center bully, one fullback plays up and the other remains back. Usually the left fullback is up as she protects the non-stick side of the center-half. From then on, the fullback on whose side the play is on moves up and down the field marking her inner, trying to intercept a pass to her, or tackling immediately if she receives the ball. The other fullback plays back deeply, near the edge of the circle, placing herself constantly between the line of the ball and the goal. Why? For two reasons, mainly: one, to intercept any through pass and two, if any forward or forwards break through the rest of the defense, she is waiting at the edge of the circle to make one more tackle before a shot is made for the goal.

If the play is in the attacking end of the field and on your side, how far you play up the field depends entirely on your own speed, the speed of the opposing forward line, and your confidence in your halfbacks. You should, under most situations, be able to move up as far as the 25-yard line in backing up your team.

When the play is at the opposite end of the field, the fullback who is up remains so until the play makes a definite change to the other side and her team seems once again to be on the defense. Then she must run quickly back and towards the deep center prepared for any through pass which might be made by her opponents. If the through pass goes to the opposite inner, the covering fullback should not rush forward to tackle until her partner is well on her way back to a covering position. If she moved up immediately, an intelligent forward would place the ball right between the two fullbacks and rush through to retrieve it, leaving the goalkeeper at the mercy of one or more forwards. Remember that no goal can be scored until the attacking team can get to the circle.

If the wing on your side gets past the halfback, do not rush out to tackle in an attempt to be helpful. A wing who has passed her opposing halfback is also capable of passing you, and your team would then be without two of its defense players even before the play had reached the edge of the circle. Give your halfback a chance to recover and pursue her opposing wing. The wing, knowing she is being pursued, will undoubtedly pass. You must be prepared for this. Do not let the pass reach the inner if you can help it but, if it does, tackle immediately. If the wing does not pass and reaches the edge of the circle without having been tackled by the halfback, you must be in position to do so before a shot for the goal is taken. It is true that at this crucial moment you have left your inner free but your entire defense will be aware of your predicament. If, in their judgment, the wing half will be unable to catch up in time to prevent the shot, your other fullback will move across ready to mark your inner, and in turn her halfback can move in to mark the other inner. Further along another form of defense for this situation will be explained for, as play becomes more advanced, you will have a covering fullback even in the circle. In the beginning stages, however, it is much wiser for each defense to mark her own player in the circle, and marking means being within stick's reach of your opponent.

Fullbacks and halfbacks should remember that although their objective is to prevent a forward from taking a shot for the goal, once the ball is underway it is then the goalkeeper's ball! Too often fullbacks, particularly, try to stop these shots, thereby unsighting the goalkeeper or even, unfortunately, deflecting the ball in such a way that the goalkeeper cannot prevent the ball from being rushed in by an oncoming forward. Let the goalkeeper stop the shot and attempt her clear. The fullbacks and the halfbacks should be ready to assist by receiving a clear from the goalkeeper if she cannot pass it through to her own forwards.

LEFT FULLBACK. Playing on the left has both its compensations and difficulties. It is easier to drive to the left, an asset when in or near the circle. However, elsewhere a strong drive to the right is necessary for distributing the play. Quick footwork and a good hit could result in sending the ball to your right wing or right inner. This is an excellent move.

Although you should be proficient in all tackles, the circular tackle is a necessity. For example, if your inner has passed you, particularly in the defending half of your field, by doing a circular tackle you will be able to take the ball away from her, moving towards the outside of the field rather than having the ball move towards the goal.

As you approach for a straight on tackle on the edge of the circle or in it, and there is a possibility that you may not get the ball, at least try to force your opponent to dodge to your non-stick side. Not only will this make the angle of her shot for a goal more difficult, but also your left halfback should be there to pick up the dodge.

RIGHT FULLBACK. Practice particularly the tackles from the right in order to carry the ball away from the center of the field. As you approach for a straight-on tackle at the edge or inside the circle, protect your non-stick side by approaching or waiting at a slight angle. Your opposing left inner may then do a pull to the left dodge, which makes her angle for shooting more difficult. If the dodge gets by you, the covering fullback or the center-half may lunge to pick up the dodge before the inner can shoot. Your right half will not be able to assist as the ball will be to her non-stick side, and any move she makes would bring the ball more towards the center of the goal.

As you move to cover when your left fullback is up near the play, you must shift over further than the left back needs to in a similar situation because of your non-stick side. As you progress beyond the beginning stage and cover in the circle as well, moving far enough over to have the ball on your stick side is *most important. Never drive the ball across the goal.*

GOALKEEPER. (Figure 28) This position can be most exciting if you are warmly and suitably dressed and protected, and if your defense allows you to play as you should: all shots for the goal are yours. Your greatest thrills will come when you can clear the ball in such a way

Figure 28

that it will result in a move by your own team down the field, culminating in a goal. Do not be content just to stop a ball but be aggressive with your clears. The direction of your clears will depend upon the oncoming forwards and your own defense.

You are the only person who is allowed to use her feet on the ball and whose stick is secondary. It is very important that your feet be well protected with kickers, and that your goal pads fit so you can move quickly and easily, with great mobility through your knees and ankles. Gloves are recommended, particularly one for your left hand as you are allowed to catch or at least "put away" any ball coming high. Your stick should be held part way down with your right hand. It can in this position be used to reach for a ball or for a short quick one-handed drive. The stick is really of secondary importance and is used as an emergency measure. Your feet and legs are primary and well padded as they are, are far more effective in stopping and clearing than the small head of your stick.

44

You should move in the shape of a semicircle in front of your goal, thereby diminishing the number of available angles for shots at the goal. To help orient yourself to your position, use your stick to mark lightly a semicircle or two straight lines out from your goal posts. As a special hint, by keeping your goal pads dazzling white, not only will you look smarter, but you set up a lovely target that forwards find hard not to aim for.

As you move, keep your knees easily flexed, your feet as close together as possible and your stick on the ground. As the play comes down the field, shift in relation to the path of the ball. Never stand and wait on the goal line except when a corner is awarded, when the rule specifies that you must stand behind the goal line until the hit is taken. If the play is straight ahead, then out you move in front of the goal; standing on the line would give your opponents a large opening on either side of you. If the play is to your left stay fairly close to that goal post with your stick ready for anything that goes to your right. If the ball is approaching from the right, you, too, must move to your right but be constantly aware of the vulnerability of your non-stick side, for forwards will, whenever possible, aim for your left.

When you can move into a ball before it can be reached by a forward, do so and clear immediately. If ever that horrible but rare moment arrives when you are alone and faced by a forward coming in to shoot, do not just stand back and wait. Even if she is at the edge of the circle, move out and try to block her shot or intercept her dodge. You should make yourself as wide as possible while keeping your feet fairly close together and in the path of the ball. Watch her ball control carefully. If the ball is well off her stick, get to it first. By coming out, you both hurry her shot and decrease the vulnerable area of the goal. However, remember that should you move outside the circle, you lose the special privileges of using your legs and feet to propel the ball.

You must never kick any ball with the toe of your boot as this will make the ball rise. This is called dangerous kicking for it will intimidate an attack and a penalty corner may well be called against your team. Clear with the inside of your foot.

If the shot for the goal is a hard one, and if you have time before the shot can be rushed, trap it by flexing your knees as the ball hits your pads. The ball should then be right in front of you, ready to be cleared in any direction. If the ground is bumpy, thereby making the path of the ball more difficult to judge, it is safer to stop it before clearing. If the shot is being rushed, however, the clear must take place

45

immediately. The clear is executed with a short, quick backswing and follow-through, keeping your foot along the ground; the tension in your leg and foot gives the necessary power. At the end of the clear your weight should be over the opposite foot. In all stops and clears keep your head steady and over the ball.

What should the goalkeeper practice? For general agility, practice some of the techniques described in this last chapter, wearing your kickers and pads—strenuous and hard work, yes, but so good for teaching you to move quickly and easily and with balance. It is very important that you learn to bully while dressed in pads and kickers, for if a penalty bully should be called against you, you are not allowed to remove them. Practice bullies five yards in front of the goal, the spot where a penalty bully would be taken.

For your position there are specific practices. Dribble using the inside of your feet, first one foot and then the other. This is very similar to the technique used by a soccer player. Find a wall and kick a tennis ball against it, sometimes stopping its rebound with both feet and then kicking, sometimes kicking immediately. Become equally adept with each foot and leg. As the rest of the players are educating their left hands and arms in order to control the stick, you must be developing your less skillful leg in clearing.

Have a teammate shoot balls at you in rapid fire at different angles from the edge of the circle, not waiting until you have cleared one before she hits the next. Another practice is to have a ball shot and another forward moving in with the shot. Can you clear it before she arrives?

Work with three or four forwards, each with several balls, standing at various places at the edge of the circle, shooting in turn, but still hurrying you. Have the forwards move in closer using push passes, scoops and flicks, the latter two particularly for your judgment of a ball in the air and for the use of your hand as well as your legs. Never lift your stick above shoulder level in an attempt to stop a ball.

You may not hold your feet motionless behind the ball. Have a forward continually push the ball into your feet and you try to get the ball clear no matter how small the movement of your feet.

As you play, you will devise ways of practicing which will be beneficial, for you will soon know your own strengths and weaknesses. It will be wise to analyze, after each goal is scored, where you may have erred; there is no end to this learning experience.

An agile, active, graceful goalkeeper is a joy to watch and an object of admiration to all.

4

Frequent Game Situations

FREE HITS

A free hit is awarded when an opponent commits a foul anywhere on the field outside the circle, or if an attack player makes a foul in the circle. On the field, the free hit is taken where the foul occurred, but if it is awarded in the circle, the defense may place the ball anywhere within the circle, even bringing it to the edge to gain as much advantage as possible. This choice should be a beneficial one. Not only may the free hit be taken rapidly, but also it provides an opportunity to change play from what may have been an overworked side of the field.

A free hit is meant to be an advantage to the team to which it is awarded, but it can become one only if it is taken quickly and intelligently. It must not be a "hit-and-hope" type of play. Instant awareness of where the ball is when the whistle blows makes for quicker action. If there is a doubt as to which side committed the foul and where the ball should be placed, look at the official. She will be standing opposite the place where the foul occurred and her arm will be pointing in the direction the hit is to be taken. Try from the very beginning to recognize the fouls which are called by the official. The player who rarely needs to look towards the official when the whistle is blown is not only a pleasure to umpire for but an asset to her team because of her alertness and awareness of the play.

The rule states that all other players must be five yards from the ball, and the player taking the hit must hit or push the ball along the ground. The ball may not be lifted in any way. Once the player has touched the ball, no matter how little, she may not touch it again until it has been played by someone else.

Let us first consider points to be remembered by the team awarded the free hit. The player taking the hit, particularly if she is a defense player and near the circle, should never hit the ball towards the center of the field where it might be intercepted. The through pass is of course ideal, if the space is there and the accuracy and direction allow a teammate to get to it. As the forwards move to get free or to create spaces, the defense also should be prepared to assist. Halfbacks and fullbacks can help the hitter by suddenly moving into a position level with the ball. A quick, flat or direct pass right to the stick of one of these who will immediately send it ahead can often create the space which is needed. Wings can often drop back quickly and suddenly and, if used immediately, can help to make a free hit count. The player taking the hit has the advantage of being able to disguise its direction until the last moment.

Now for the team against whom the hit is awarded. As your opponents move quickly to get free and to get the hit off as fast as possible, you in turn must become completely defensive. Forwards should immediately move to mark their opposing forwards and the defense should move rapidly to fill the spaces.

CORNERS

Whether the corner is a short or a long one, it is a penalty against the defending team. It can be a considerable advantage to the attacking team if it is aware of the importance of the initial hit from the player on the end line to the player who receives it and shoots for the goal. As mentioned before, a ball can travel faster than any player, and in good hockey, the ball can travel at lightning speed. The player taking the corner hit should make the ball travel smoothly and accurately to the person chosen to receive it, and in turn the receiver must have the ability to stop the ball "dead" on her stick and shoot immediately, dodge and shoot, or pass to another forward who will shoot.

One often hears the remark, "every corner should be a goal"; however, all too rarely does a goal in fact materialize. When the initial shot for goal, because of its accuracy and speed, results in a score, a defending team can do little but admire it.

To return to the average initial shot for goal which so often does not result in a score. If the other forwards would immediately follow up that initial shot of their teammate, goals would be more frequent. As the player receives the corner hit, the inside forwards should watch for the backswing of her drive and be on their way with the ball, or perhaps even a step ahead, ready to rush through the oncoming defense, arriving

Evaluation Questions

with sticks down to prevent the goalkeeper from clearing the ball. Fast and determined forwards approaching from various angles will get to the ball as it rebounds from the goalkeeper's pads. The unsettling effect on a goalkeeper can be gauged by forwards if they will remember their own feelings when an opponent rushes at them and hurries their play. Imagine, then, how much worse it is for the goalkeeper when she has not one but two or three players rushing at her!

Now why is a corner awarded, and how is it decided whether it is to be a long or a short corner (penalty corner)? A long corner is given when the ball goes over the end line outside of the goal posts, having glanced off the stick of a defensive player or off the pads of the goalkeeper unintentionally. The umpire can easily determine this by noting the movement of the player with her stick or the goalkeeper with her legs. The intention of the player involved was obviously to keep the ball in play, but fortune was against her. Because of her effort to keep the ball on the field, the penalty should not be as great, and thus the award to the opposing team is, and should be, less of a potential threat. The corner is taken on the side of the field where the ball went out. The ball is placed either on the end line five yards from the corner or five yards up the outside alley line. The five yards are easily judged as that is the width of the alley.

A penalty or short corner is awarded when a defender fouls in the circle, or a defense player has hit, or the goalkeeper has kicked, the ball over the end line outside the goal posts intentionally. The penalty against the defending team should therefore be more severe. The ball is now placed ten yards from the goal post on the side chosen by the attack-

49

ing team. The ten yards is easily determined because the edge of the circle, as it connects with the end line, is fifteen yards from the goal post.

Mention has been made above, in the case of both corners, about the ball going over the end line outside the goal posts. This applies only to balls last touched by a defense player on the defending side of the 25-yard line. If the ball is touched by the stick of the attacking team within the circle, glances off the stick or the legs of a defense player and goes between the goal posts, a goal is scored.

Attacking Team—The rule states that the ball must be placed on the line, but the player taking the hit may stand on the line, over it, or behind it. She may, and she would be wise to, be behind the line and then step into her drive. The rules do not specify which player must take this initial hit, but most often the wing on that side does so. It is important that the player taking the corner hit immediately return to an onside position *before* the shot for the goal is made to prevent a foul from being called against her team.

The attacking center-half may either be on the edge of the circle acting as another potential shooter of a goal or she may hover just behind the player who is about to receive the corner hit, backing her up. The other halfbacks are outside the circle, the one on the side on which the corner hit is being taken, up a little farther than the halfback on the other side. Their effort must be to intercept any pass from the opposing team and either give it back to their forwards or take it to the edge of the circle and shoot, allowing their forwards to do the rushing

If you are the person receiving the hit from the corner, do not move in to meet the ball, but calmly wait for it on the edge of the circle as this will increase the distance your defense player must move in order to get her stick on the ball. If the ball has been mis-hit or is slow in moving, you must then, of course, move in and move fast. Remember that the player receiving the corner hit must first control the ball before shooting.

Defending Team. You are now aware of the problems facing you in this particular play. There are six of you opposing as many as eight members of the attacking team. You can receive no help from your five forwards who must stand on their 25-yard line during the corner and remain there until either the ball has come out of the circle or has been touched by one of your opponents in the circle.

Before the corner hit may be taken, you must all, including the goalkeeper, stand with feet and stick behind the end line. Make sure you come out on the ball and stick side of your opponent. Also remember that speed counts, and your body and feet, as you wait for the corner hit, should be poised, ready for a sprint. When you move out, do so quickly with your sticks moving lightly along the ground, not an easy thing to do.

Have faith in your goalkeeper! Do not linger back to help her defend the goal. Your duty is to stop the opposing forwards from shooting; your goalkeeper will stop the shot if your opponents are successful in evading your sticks. If you linger back, not only will you not be doing your job but you will block the goalkeeper's view. If, by chance, a ball should rise on its way to the goal and you are dithering halfway between your opponent and the goal, you are in a dangerous position.

If you are faced with—and you will be as your opposing forwards and halfbacks become more skillful and more determined to score—the predicament of more attack than defense players, you will always tackle the free player who is on your stick side and about to shoot. If this power of attack is near the edge of the circle, your own forwards, particularly the inside ones, can drop back, once it is legal for them to move, and help to tackle back. It is important, however, that they do not muddle the defense. Perhaps it would be safer to say that your own center forward should drop back to tackle her opposing center-half if that center-half is a potential danger; and your own inner on the side where the ball is should drop back to tackle the wing half who may be preparing to shoot, or who is constantly intercepting every pass your defense is trying to get through to your forwards.

5

Defense Play
Further Defined

In the beginning stage, each defense player plays only her own opponent and the only shifting is done by the fullbacks, one up and one back, when the play is outside the circle, but level once play is in the circle. Eventually there comes that time when the weakness of such a defense is made evident for the opposing team is able to come through it time and time again. When this happens, the moment has arrived to consider the next stage. (The forwards would do well to study this next stage in order to try to outwit it.) The most important thing to remember —and this by all players on the field—is that in the system discussed here, there is always a free player: the one farthest from the ball, usually the wing.

To say there is only one system of defense would be an untruth. How to play defense is one of the greatest conversation pieces in hockey, and many ideas have merit. There is no set position for each situation. You must think for yourselves, react to situations as they occur, and play as a team, not as individuals.

Good forwards are unpredictable in their passing, their movements are quick and disguised, and they have great speed. These qualities make a forward, and it is against these that your defense must plan.

Perhaps anticipation should be considered now. Although we often hear the term "game sense," and some players seem to have it and others don't, anticipation can be cultivated. It is not a magic quality; it is simply being prepared for anything. It means thinking ahead, but not moving so you will warn an opponent. It means helping other defense players at the correct moment. It means getting to the right place at the right time.

If you could develop this type of anticipation and cultivate complete concentration, many problems would be solved. As a defense player, you should expect the worst and hope for the best. The longer you play the more you will realize that you have your own favorite position and others have theirs, but each of you must be aware of the responsibilities and positioning of the others.

Marking means being within stick's reach of an opponent in order to move to intercept any pass that will come to her, or to tackle as soon as she receives the ball. *Covering* means placing oneself so as to intercept any through pass or tackle any free player as a last resort. For fullbacks a fairly general description would be between the ball and the goal. This system of defense is based upon the philosophy of "attacking" halfbacks, for a team is only as strong as its halfback line. You read earlier that fullbacks never play square; this is also true of the three halfbacks. Except in the defending circle, they are usually on a diagonal line, the two closest to the play farther up than the one away from the side the ball is on.

At the center bully, the left half should be as far out as the wings, and the right should play in slightly—each protecting her non-stick side. Their positions should be fairly deep in order to be able to intercept a long through pass to the wings; it is far better on the initial play for a halfback to move forward to play the ball than to have to turn and chase it. Against a team which lacks hitting power at the time of the bully, the depth of the wing halves is not necessary. The center-half backs up the bully. The left fullback usually plays up, protecting the non-stick side of the center-half. Also, her opposing center forward is facing in her direction and therefore is more apt to hit in that direction. The right fullback plays deeper, more towards a covering position. If the play goes to the right, she will immediately move farther back and over to the center; but if the ball does travel to her side, she has less distance to move up on the attack, as soon as her left fullback begins to retreat to the covering position. Should the opposing team consistently send the ball to the left following the bully, by all means start with the right fullback up.

The strategy of both teams is based on the realization that the player with the ball is marked. Her teammates on either side should also be marked by their immediate opponents. The position of the two remaining defense players, namely the covering fullback and the wing half farthest from the ball, is of primary importance. The wing halfback plays a key role, both on the attack and on the defense.

On the attack her positioning, although backing up her own forwards, is still farther back than the wing half on whose side the ball is. Her primary task is to be prepared to intercept any ball which might come towards the opposing inner or wing, as her own fullback is deep in the defending half of the field, prepared to intercept the long through pass. In the defending half of the field, particularly from the 25-yard line back, she will mark more closely the opposing inner as long as her fullback continues in a covering position. Once the play moves to her side of the field, her opposing wing becomes her immediate objective as the fullbacks begin their shift, and the wing halfback on the opposite side moves in to mark the opposing inner.

As play moves into the circle, but still near its edge, more advanced players will see the necessity for a covering fullback. Her position is difficult but challenging. It is difficult because she must not either unsight her goalkeeper or crowd her in any way, yet she must be ready for the dodge or little through pass which goes behind the rest of her defense. She must be quick to pounce on the ball and clear.

Once play moves deep into the circle each defense player must mark her own opponent, with her back to the goal she is defending. Any ball which now gets behind this defense very definitely belongs to the goalkeeper.

(The wing farthest from the ball on the attacking team is free. This should certainly give ideas to the attack. If this free wing would drop back slightly behind her other forwards, a well directed pass should reach her. Such a pass could send the opposing defense scuttling across to change their positions of marking and covering, but a ball well hit can travel faster than any player. More use of the wings will keep wing halves on the move and less able to cope with the inner whose fullback is covering at the time. Try always to catch the opposing defense during their methodical shifts. Another factor that must now be more apparent is the importance of forwards constantly moving and spacing themselves in the circle. Such activity will also not only keep the defense spread out but also divide its attention between the players and the ball.)

Wing halfbacks are most assuredly the main link on the attack and on the defense. A halfback who hovers between an inner and a wing will be of no use in either situation. A good inner would be delighted with such carelessness. Should this happen, however, get back to your wing. Your fullback should be ready!

Defense players must be on the move continually because every time the ball is played, the path along which it might travel changes. Positioning, anticipation and intercepting are all based on possible angles. To improve your anticipation note that a player with a slow backswing cannot disguise the direction of her drive; and a player who must hop or skip in preparation for a drive telegraphs her intention.

Basic judgments of defense players can be governed by the following:

1. As a defense player attempts a tackle, the rest of her defense should be prepared for what might happen should she miss, or if the player with the ball passes before being tackled.

2. If a defense player is dodged, the next nearest defense should not move in immediately but should give the passed player a chance to recover and tackle back. (Exception—at the edge of the circle before the shot is made for the goal, another defense player must attempt to get the ball.)

These two examples assumes that the player with the ball has control of it. If a ball is well ahead of a player any defender who can get to it and get rid of it before an opponent can catch up should do so. It will save time and energy, and it will start an attacking move for the team. On the other side of the ledger, *any forward who can get to a free ball should do so with purpose and speed and her other forwards should adjust their positions and spacing accordingly.*

The important thing for defenders to remember is that when a fullback is covering, the half should move in to the inner. How closely she plays to this inner depends upon whether the play is in the defending or the attacking half of the field. This, combined with understanding and teamwork, will result in a formidable defense against any team.

6

Better Players
Master These Techniques

PUSH PASS

A push pass, or a flick, can be overused by players who are not quick enough to get their feet up to the ball and hit. The push pass is a valuable stroke, particularly advantageous if either the surface is very fast or if the ground is very bumpy, and it makes receiving drives difficult. The push pass can be made to cover little territory or a distance of well over twenty-five yards. In a drive, the stick is removed from behind the ball and in that instant you may be robbed of it but in the push pass, the stick never leaves the ball. The pass is performed with either foot forward and it can be made to travel in almost any direction. The pass is often more easily received because its path is smoother and it has great advantage for forwards in the circle who wish to get the shot away before being tackled.

Place the right hand a little farther down your stick than usual. Put the ball several feet ahead of you and place your stick against it. With a strong forward motion of the arms and keeping the stick as perpendicular to the ground for as long as possible, takes a long step or lunge, bending your knee, and push the ball at the same time. (Figure 29 (1) (2)) For a push pass of any distance, your finishing position will make you feel as though you are falling forward. Because you are low to the ground at the end of the push pass, you must avoid letting the toe of the stick come up as you will make sticks. As you practice, think of pushing something much heavier than a hockey ball. Once you have the feeling of pushing the ball, dribble and push first straight ahead and then to the left and to the right. Strive for accuracy.

Figure 29 (1)   *Figure 29 (2)*

A wing or an inner with a strong push pass can be used most successfully on a corner. A push can travel at great speed and the player receiving the push pass at the edge of the circle may have a greater advantage in getting her shot away if she does not have to worry about a ball
which might be bouncy.

FLICK

This stroke is a combination of the push pass and the scoop. It
can travel the distance of a push pass and even farther, and it has the
height of the scoop. It is excellent for shooting within the circle and
also for passing when there is an opponent's stick between you and the
person to whom you wish to pass. Too high a flick can be dangerous.
As with the scoop, the higher the ball off the ground, the easier it is
for an opponent to stop it with either her hand or stick. A flick that
just leaps over an opponent's stick is much more difficult to judge, however, and this is why it is such a good shot for goal. Do not overuse the
flick, for it can be very difficult to receive. It may still be in the air
just off the ground as your teammate attempts to receive it, or it might
have quite a spin on it.

The beginning of the stroke is similar to the push pass. Arms and
body weight play their part for distance. Added to this, however, is a
powerful action of the wrists which, at the end of the stroke, flick and
lift the stick and the ball. The follow-through is long and stretched,
with the blade of the stick facing upwards. For some people the flick
is difficult to learn, perhaps because of misjudging the amount of energy
this stroke needs.

Is this grip correct for the dribble? the push pass? the drive? the flick?

Evalution Questions

GRIPPING THE STICK

The following hint may help. At the start, instead of placing your stick behind the ball, place the face of the stick to the side and against the ball. Now as you push, your wrists will have to act quickly as you bring the stick around the ball to face in the direction you wish the flick to go. It is almost a circular motion, "cuddling" the ball before you release it.

REVERSE STICK DRIVE

The ball is ahead of you and you have no time to get your feet up to it or even beyond it to hit the ball to your right. Keep your hands together as for any drive and twist your wrists so that the back of the left hand and the palm of the right hand face the ground. Take a short quick backswing and follow through, using more wrist action than arm swing and send the ball directly to the right or diagonally back. (Figure 30) Your aim must be good because you are using only the toe of the stick. Individuals will vary greatly in their execution of this drive. It can often be used as a surprise move, but is more likely to be used when a forward is saving a ball from going over either the side or the end line, and when she is well ahead of her opponent.

RIGHT LUNGE

This tackle or spoil stroke takes a great deal of practice and control because you are attempting to play the ball with just the toe of your stick. The action comes primarily in the wrists and therefore it is not a true lunge with a long sweep of the stick.

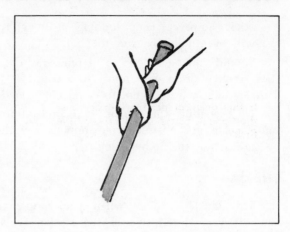

Diagram C:

GRIPPING THE STICK

Your opponent is on your right, and either you cannot get on a level with the ball to do a circular tackle or perhaps it is important that you spoil her intentions quickly. Reverse your stick as you do for the reverse stick drive and, as you run along beside her, decide which of two possibilities you should choose. (Figure 31) If the ball is far enough off

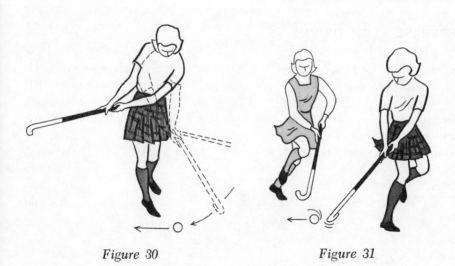

Figure 30   *Figure 31*

your opponent's stick so that you can give it a slight tap, thereby pushing it to her right and out of line with her stick, do so. Be careful to remove your stick quickly so as not to trip her. If the ball is kept very close to

59

her stick, however, keep tapping at it with short quick taps, hoping she will eventually overrun the ball.

Should you be successful in removing the ball from your opponent's stick, remember as you move to retrieve it that she will tackle back. Turn in such a way as not to come between her and the ball.

In executing this tackle two precautions are necessary to avoid fouling. Do not obstruct your opponent with your right shoulder and be careful not to hit her stick.

THE JAB

This tackle is done when your opponent is on your right. The name is very descriptive of the stroke. It is done with the left arm in order to avoid obstruction with the right shoulder. The wrist must be kept firm and the arm straight. The stroke is performed with the shaft of the stick as parallel to the ground as possible and the blade of the stick facing upward. Because of the weight of the stick in this position and because this tackle must be attempted while running at top speed, the left wrist and arm must be strong and the stroke must be performed with great control. It requires a long reach as you attempt to lift the ball from in front of your opponent's stick. Whether or not you are successful, be careful not to dangle your stick in front of your opponent. Beware of either tripping her or interfering with her stick.

Rules of the Game

Rules are designed for safety, courtesy and fair play. Specifically they tell you how to put the ball in play, how to score, what is legal and illegal play and the penalties for violations. Many of these have been included in this text but space does not permit more than the basic elements so the Official Field Hockey Guide and Rulebook should be consulted.

1. Center bullies are taken at the beginning of the game, the second half and after each goal is scored.

2. Bullies occur also at the time of a double foul; when an accident has happened in which no foul was made; if the ball goes over the side line off the sticks of two opponents simultaneously.

3. Should the ball go over the side line off the stick of a player, a roll-in is awarded to the opposing team. For any infringement of a roll-in, the roll-in is then taken by the other team. (Exception—should the player taking the roll-in not have her stick in her hand, a free hit is awarded to the other team.)

4. Should the ball be sent over the end line by the attacking team, the defense is awarded a free hit 15 yards from the end line *opposite* the spot where the ball crossed the line.

5. For any foul outside the two circles, a free hit is awarded to the opposing team where the foul occurred. All players must be five yards from the player taking the hit. The fouls are: sticks; obstruction; offside; dangerous hitting; charging; advancing; hitting sticks.

6. In the circle, if a foul is made by the attack, a free hit is awarded to the defense and the ball may be placed anywhere in the circle. Usually it is taken at the edge of the circle.

7. A long corner is awarded if the ball glances off the stick of a defense player anywhere on the defending side of the 25-yard line, or off the pads of the goalkeeper in the circle. The corner must be taken on the side where the ball crossed the line.

8. A short or penalty corner is awarded when a defense player fouls in the circle or sends the ball intentionally over the end line. The attacking team may choose the side on which to take the corner.

9. A penalty bully is awarded when a foul occurs which, in the opinion of the umpire, prevented a goal from being scored. Although it is more often the goalkeeper who is involved, it could be any member of the defense. During the penalty bully all players other than the two taking the bully must stand beyond the 25-yard line and remain there. The bully is begun and ended by the official's whistle. If the defense player is successful the game is restarted by a bully on the 25-yard line.

10. No player in her attacking half of the field may be ahead of one of her own team who is in possession of the ball, before the ball has been hit or rolled in, *unless* there are three opponents between her and the goal. (The goalkeeper can be included in the three.) This is the rule of *offside*. For any infringement of this rule, a free hit is awarded to the opposing team, to be taken *on the spot where the player was called offside*. In the circle, the free hit by the defense may be taken anywhere.

Do not be surprised if the umpire does not blow her whistle at every infringement of the rules. She may be "holding the whistle" to see if, on the next play, the team which would have been given the free hit or corner gains more advantage than if play had been stopped and the penalty awarded. The main purpose is to let the game "flow" and much is left to the discretion of the umpire. You therefore should play to the whistle and not stop automatically when a foul or violation occurs. Should an official miss a foul which resulted in a goal for the team of the offender, however, sportsmanship demands acknowledgment by the player who fouled.

8

Facts for Enthusiasts and Unwritten Laws

If you can purchase your own stick, do so. Once you have become accustomed to its balance and weight, every other stick will seem odd and unfamiliar. Indian head sticks are now more popular than the traditional English style because of their maneuverability. As equipment must be cared for, be sure you know the type of wood of which it is made. Sticks made of ash must be waxed to prevent moisture from being absorbed into the wood; those made of mulberry must be oiled.

If you are a real enthusiast, poor weather need not prevent you from practicing. To protect a gym floor, place a sock on the end of your stick, cover an old ball, set up obstacles to dribble in and out of, to dodge or to shoot at, or a combination of all. Practice on your weaknesses instead of the things you do well and hence enjoy more.

In the east, midwest and now in California, boarding and day camps have been established for those who desire a concentrated period of practice and play.

Arrive well in time for a game in order to be thoroughly warmed up before begining to play. Forwards should make sure that their goalkeeper has practice before the game.

Your appearance should be impeccable from head to foot and a replica of each of your teammates. A uniform develops esprit de corps and also makes it easier to find your teammates during the game.

Your captain is chosen because you respect her leadership, her ability, her knowledge of the game, and because you are willing to take criticism from her. Once play is underway it is she and she alone who quietly gives any coaching hints. Occasionally in the circle your goalkeeper might say "mark" or "mine." A good team plays in silence, each player striving for concentration and anticipation. In good hockey, there is no coaching from the side lines nor is there chatter on the field. There are those who think that if all is silent, there is no enthusiasm and no esprit de corps among the players. Yet in doubles play, in either tennis or badminton, one does not hear continuous conversation among players. If you are playing hard and fast, you will not have the energy or time to coach everyone else on the field. It will be enough to play your own position and listen to *occasional* advice from your captain.

Before the game begins it is customary to shake hands with your opponent and introduce yourself. At the end of the game you should once again shake hands and thank her. Either your captain or the team as a whole should thank the two officials also.

During the game neither by word or by look should you question an official or show disapproval of her decision. As no player is perfect, neither is any official; as you try never to foul, the umpire tries never to miscall or miss one.

When the game is over the participants' conduct is also important. If your team has lost, excuses should not be made as this places the victors in a most uncomfortable position. Rather learn to recognize your mistakes and be determined to do better the next time. The winners, too, have a responsibility not to increase the hurt of the losers. Learning how to win and to lose are equally important.

The Lore of the Game

HISTORY

As early as 500 B.C., there were games which might well have been fore-runners of field hockey. The game might have originated in Persia, have been brought from there to Greece and Rome, and then taken by the Romans to the British Isles at the time of the Gallic Wars.

Through the centuries hockey must have passed through many phases in its development and, until 1887, when the first field hockey club for women was founded in England, the game was played only by men.

Hockey on Staten Island, led by the wife of the British Ambassador, is mentioned in the 1890's. Not until 1901, however, was the game to be formally introduced to the United States and to begin to make its contribution to the lives of so many young people. Miss Constance M. K. Apple-bee, a young Englishwoman with energy, enthusiasm and belief in such a team sport for young women, traveled to many eastern colleges in that year, carrying with her twenty-two sticks and a ball. In 1963, sixty-two years later, the "Apple," as she is affectionately known, fully realized her faith and teaching when the United States Field Hockey Association played hostess to the International Federation of Women's Hockey As-sociations. Delegates from 26 and teams from 22 countries participated.

Through the years both rules and dress have undergone marked changes. In the beginning each area wrote its own rules, but eventually the English rules were generally adopted. As for dress, in 1901 the recom-mended uniform was a long skirt, six inches from the ground, knicker-bockers, and flannel shirts.

Skirts . . . (should be) of light woolen material, made plainly like a bicycling skirt. Petticoats should not be worn, for however short, they are awkward to run in; knickerbockers fastening at the knee should be substituted. The shirt or blouse, made of flannel to prevent risk of chills, must be loose (this does not necessitate untidyness), neat fitting and made after the uniform club pattern. The goalkeeper and fullbacks will find sweaters or coats made in the club colors useful on cold days. Keeping comfort and play in view the hair should be properly fixed; opportunities are so often lost by a player who has to continually attend to hairpins instead of the ball. ("Field Hockey for Women" 1901 Spaulding's Athletic Library Group VI, No. 154, N. Y. American Sports Publishing Company, 1901, p. 11.)

Enthusiasm led to the forming of the United States Field Hockey Association (USFHA). A nonprofit organization run by women on a volunteer basis, its sole purpose is to spread the knowledge and pleasure of the game and to offer opportunities for competition at all levels.

10

Playing the Game

Your hockey need not stop when you leave college, but may lead to even keener competition and greater rewards. Under the guidance and assistance of the USFHA, there are local clubs and associations which you may join regardless of your ability. In the official United States Field Hockey and Lacrosse Guide, published under the sponsorship of the Division of Girls and Women's Sports (DGWS), can be found the name and address of the executive secretary who, upon request, will let you know the location of the club nearest you.

Perhaps one day you may have the opportunity to play against a team from a foreign country, representing either your local association, your section or your country. No words can describe the challenge or the thrill of such an experience.

Because the USFHA is a member country of the International Federation of Women's Hockey Associations (IFWHA), there are reciprocal tours which make available opportunities for travel and friendships under circumstances impossible for the ordinary tourist. To give you some idea of the scope of this exciting game, teams from the United States have played in the British Isles, Denmark, Germany, Belgium, France, Holland, Switzerland, Spain, Australia, New Zealand, South Africa, the Fiji Islands, Jamaica, Trinidad and British Guiana. Other member countries of the IFWHA are Argentina, Austria, Canada, Ceylon, Hong Kong, India, Malaysia, Uganda and Zambia.

For all of you who go on to play regardless of the level you will eventually reach—and who can predict now what that may be—a rewarding experience is promised.

Figure 32

For all those players of the past, for those of the present and for those who have yet to play the game, the following quotation must surely epitomize the spirit of play and the reward one receives from participation:

We have looked into the past and ahead to the future. We have reviewed the present that we share here, and little remains to be said. But, a word in conclusion: We are a small group in a huge and complex world,—insignificant perhaps, if measured by size, and if judged by prominence, seemingly unimportant. But the world is people. Its destiny surely will be shaped by the individual,—his influence, his relationship, his conduct and his creed. And who can measure influence, or say how big or how small it will be, or judge the power of one ideal or one idea?

We are small in size but we need never be small in stature. We have something to contribute. It is important, how important we cannot know. We have learned that we can laugh together in fun and fellowship, and laughter is important. We have freely, and by mutual consent, accepted a code of rules, and law is important. We have found that we can speak to each other with words and without them, and the language of understanding is important. May we hold to those things with confidence and faith! May we always be able to look across oceans, over boundaries and barriers, and say happily and in trust: 'My friend lives there.'[1]

---

[1]Conclusion of talk by Anne Townsend as master of ceremonies at final banquet of International Field Hockey Conference—Goucher College, September 18, 1963.

Index